abdopublishing.com

Published by Abdo Kids, a division of ABDO, PO Box 398166, Minneapolis, Minnesota 55439.

Copyright © 2016 by Abdo Consulting Group, Inc. International copyrights reserved in all countries. No part of this book may be reproduced in any form without written permission from the publisher.

Printed in the United States of America, North Mankato, Minnesota.

052015

092015

Photo Credits: iStock, Shutterstock

Production Contributors: Teddy Borth, Jennie Forsberg, Grace Hansen

Design Contributors: Laura Rask, Dorothy Toth

Library of Congress Control Number: 2014958428

Cataloging-in-Publication Data

Hansen, Grace.

 Rocks / Grace Hansen.

  p. cm. -- (Geology rocks!)

ISBN 978-1-62970-909-3

Includes index.

1. Rocks--Juvenile literature.   I. Title.

552--dc23

                    2014958428

Table of Contents

Rocks

Rocks come in all shapes and sizes. Rocks are made up of one or more **minerals**. There are more than 4,000 minerals on Earth.

4

Igneous Rocks

There are three main kinds

of rocks. One is **igneous rock**.

It is made from **magma**.

6

igneous rock: granite

7

Magma is inside the Earth.
It is very hot. It cools as it
rises. It hardens into rock.
Crystals can be found
inside these rocks.

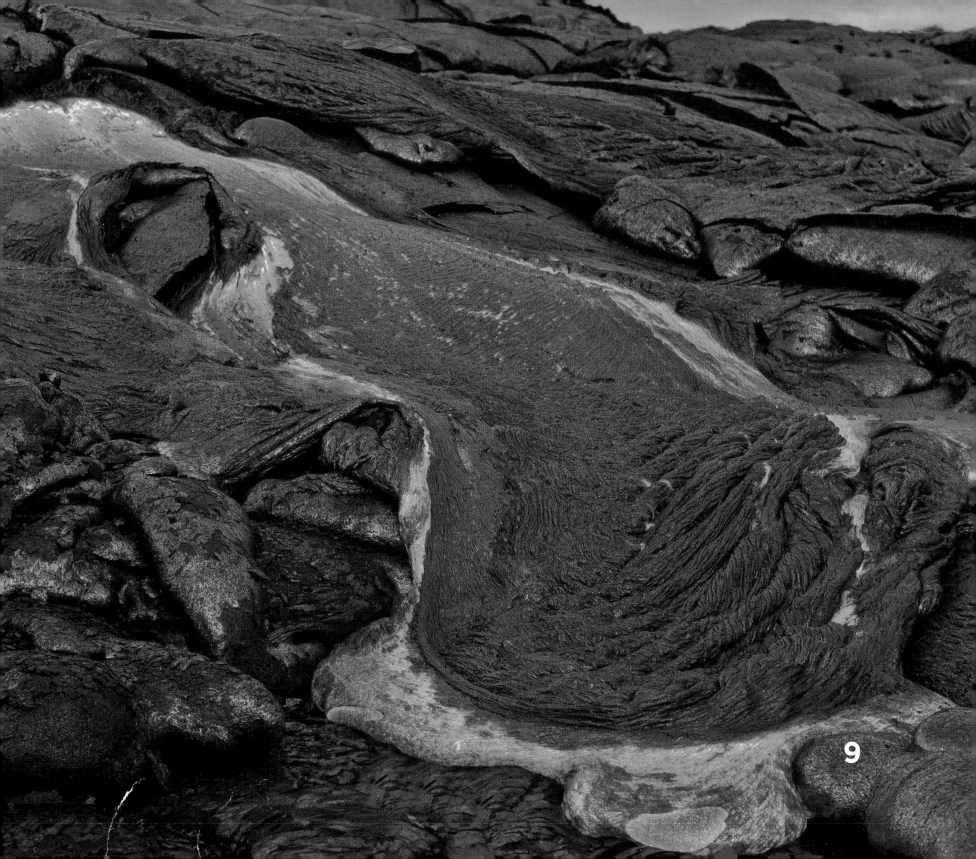

9

Sedimentary Rocks

Another kind of rock is **sedimentary rock**. It is made of many tiny rocks. Pieces of rocks pile together in layers.

10

sedimentary rock: sandstone

The weight of the pile creates pressure. **Minerals** glue the rocks together. All the tiny rocks form one large rock.

Sedimentary rock has lines in it. You can see the different layers. The Grand Canyon is one example.

14

metamorphic rock: marble

17

More Than Just Rocks

Humans have always used rocks. We use rocks as tools.

19

We use rocks to make sidewalks. We use them to build homes. We even make jewelry out of rocks!

21

Rock Types

igneous

basalt

granite

pumice

metamorphic

marble

slate

talc

sedimentary

coal

halite

limestone

22

Glossary

igneous rock – rock formed by the cooling and solidifying of magma or lava.

magma – melted rock beneath or within Earth's surface. Igneous rock is formed from it. Magma becomes lava once it reaches Earth's surface.

metamorphic rock – rock that was once one form of rock but has changed to a different rock from heat and pressure.

mineral – a substance (such as salt) that is naturally formed under the ground. It makes up rocks and other parts of nature.

sedimentary rock – rock that has formed from many tiny pieces of rocks.

Index

abdokids.com

Use this code to log on to abdokids.com and access crafts, games, videos, and more!

Abdo Kids Code:
GRK9093